A catalogue record for this book is available from the British Library

Published by Ladybird Books Ltd
A subsidiary of the Penguin Group
A Pearson Company

LADYBIRD and the device of a Ladybird are trademarks of Ladybird Books Ltd Loughborough Leicestershire UK

Adapted from Walt Disney Pictures' Hercules

Music by Alan Menken   Lyrics by David Zippel   Original score by Alan Menken

Produced by Alice Dewey and John Musker & Ron Clements   Directed by John Musker & Ron Clements

DISNEY'S
HERCULES

Ladybird

4

Hi, everybody! We're the Muses, and we've got quite a story to tell you.

Way back when the world began, some guys called the Titans were scaring everyone with storms and earthquakes and monster volcanoes. Then Zeus, the boss-man of the gods, came along. He threw those Titans in a hole and gave his own gods and goddesses jobs to do. Everyone on Earth was grateful—but those Titans were just waiting to get back at Zeus. In the meantime, though, something happened that changed everything…

Fireworks lit up the sky over Mount Olympus, home of the gods, to celebrate the arrival of Zeus and Hera's son, Hercules. It was obvious to everyone that this was no ordinary baby. He was cute and cuddly, to be sure, but he was also unbelievably strong. He could easily lift his mighty father above his head!

All the Olympian gods attended the celebration, bringing an array of amazing presents. But Zeus was not to be outdone. He spun several clouds into an adorable winged baby horse and gave it to Hercules as a present from himself and Hera. "His name is Pegasus," Zeus said, beaming, "and he's all yours, son."

6

Soon Hades, the god of the Underworld, appeared. He hated Zeus for putting him in charge of a place that was full of dead people. But Zeus was Hades' boss, after all, so Hades just smiled and handed baby Hercules a dummy shaped like a skull, with spikes sticking out of it!

Baby Hercules grabbed Hades' hand and squeezed it until Hades reeled in pain. "He's going to be the strongest of all the gods," Zeus announced proudly.

Furious, Hades went back to the Underworld to consult the Fates. These were three hideous old women who could see the past, present and future with the single eye they shared. They could also cut a person's Thread of Life, sending them straight to the Underworld.

"Is Hercules going to ruin my plan to take over Olympus?" he asked.

The Fates had mixed news for him – in eighteen years, when the planets became perfectly aligned, Hades could overthrow Zeus. "But," they added, "if Hercules fights on the side of the gods, you will fail!"

11

Hades sent his henchmen, Pain and Panic, to kidnap baby Hercules and take him to Earth. He ordered them to give him a special potion to drink, which would make him mortal. Then they could kill him.

But before Hercules finished the potion, the villains were disturbed by a passing couple. Pain and Panic, disguised as snakes, slithered towards Hercules to complete their task, but he flung them aside like playthings. Hercules was now mortal but his amazing strength remained.

"Oh, great!" whined Panic. "Hades is gonna kill us now!"

"Not if he doesn't find out," said Pain.

Now that he was mortal, Hercules could not return to Olympus. The couple on the road, Amphitryon and Alcmene, adopted him and raised him as their own. Hercules grew into a loving, devoted son.

But Hercules' uncontrolled strength often led to disaster. One day he tried to join some boys playing discus in the marketplace. They sent him away, but he jumped to catch the discus anyway. He bumped into some pillars, which crashed down, leaving the marketplace in ruins. The angry townsfolk warned Amphitryon to keep Hercules away.

Hercules was in despair. "I'll never fit in around here!" he told Amphitryon and Alcmene. "I have to find out where I *do* belong."

His parents decided to tell Hercules the truth. They showed him the gold medallion he had been wearing when they had found him.

"It has the symbol of the gods on it," Alcmene explained.

Maybe they have the answers I'm looking for, Hercules thought. Now he knew that he had to begin his quest with a visit to the temple of Zeus. Sadly, he and his parents said their farewells.

At the temple, Hercules knelt before the statue of Zeus to pray. Suddenly the enormous figure came to life!

"EEEEEOWW!" screamed Hercules, running away.

"Hey, hold on!" said Zeus. "Is that the kind of hello you give your father?"

Hercules was confused. If Zeus was his father, then Hercules must be… a god!

But Zeus explained that Hercules wasn't a god, he was human now – and humans weren't allowed on Mount Olympus.

"Isn't there anything you can do?" Hercules asked.

"I can't, but you can," Zeus told him. "You must prove yourself a true hero on Earth. Begin by seeking out Philoctetes, the trainer of heroes, on the Isle of Idra."

To help Hercules, Zeus reunited him with his old friend Pegasus.

"I won't let you down, Father!" called Hercules as he and Pegasus flew off towards Idra.

Hercules was surprised to discover that Philoctetes was a wisecracking little satyr – a half man, half goat creature. Hercules told Phil about his dream of being a hero, and asked the trainer to help him.

At first Phil refused – everyone else he'd tried to train had let him down. "A guy can take only so much disappointment," he explained.

But Hercules insisted that he was different. "Wait till you see how strong I am," he said. "I can go the distance!" He even revealed to Phil that he was the son of Zeus.

"Zeus? The big guy? Mr Lightning Bolts?" asked Phil in disbelief.

Hercules swore it was true, but Phil still refused – until Zeus sent a lightning bolt his way.

"Okay!" Phil agreed, finally convinced. "You win!"

Hercules' training began with Phil putting him through gruelling exercises. He taught him various fighting techniques, explaining how to rescue a damsel in distress, and to concentrate under pressure.

As the seasons changed, so did Hercules. He grew from an awkward youth to a skilled athlete, keen to demonstrate his abilities.

"I'm ready!" cried Hercules. "I want to battle some monsters and rescue some damsels!"

"Okay," Phil agreed. "You want a road test! We're going to Thebes."

On the way to Thebes the friends came upon Meg, a beautiful young woman who was in the clutches of a burly centaur named Nessus.

"Back off, Atlas," Meg snapped at Hercules. But eager to notch up hero points, Hercules fought the centaur anyway – and won.

With Nessus out of the way, Hercules was desperate to meet Meg. Phil was annoyed – a hero shouldn't have any distractions – and Pegasus was jealous, but Hercules tried to introduce himself. Unfortunately Meg wasn't impressed. With a casual, "Bye-bye, Wonder Boy," she left.

But now Meg was in trouble. She had to explain to her boss, Hades, that a strongman named Hercules had chased off Nessus, and she hadn't recruited the centaur for his army as she'd been ordered.

"You were supposed to kill Hercules!" Hades fumed.

"At least we made him mortal," stammered Pain and Panic.

But Hades wanted Hercules dead—so he hatched a new plot to get rid of the hero.

Meanwhile, arriving in Thebes, Hercules announced that he was the hero everyone had been waiting for. The Thebans just rolled their eyes. No hero had ever been able to stop the fires, earthquakes and floods that had plagued them.

"You'll get your chance," Phil assured Hercules. "All we need is a catastrophe."

Right on cue, Meg appeared. "Two little boys are trapped by a rock slide!" she cried. Hercules was thrilled. Here was his big break!

31

As the townsfolk crowded round the edge of the canyon, Hercules lifted a massive boulder high above his head, freeing the boys. Hercules waited, but only a few people applauded. The Thebans were a tough audience! The boys scampered up the canyon and stopped at Hades' feet – where they changed back into Pain and Panic.

Moments later, as Phil joined Hercules in the canyon, the two became aware of a strange hissing noise.

Suddenly there was a crack of lightning, and a gigantic dragonlike creature – the Hydra – emerged from a cave. As Phil ran for cover, Hercules drew his sword and prepared to do battle with the beast.

Hercules fought valiantly against the powerful creature. He attacked the Hydra with his sword, sending its head toppling to the ground.

Pain and Panic stole nervous glances at Hades, but the hot-headed god was strangely relaxed. For the Hydra wasn't dead. Three writhing heads had grown in place of the original! Hercules sliced at them with his sword, but each time he did, they multiplied!

"Forget the head-slicing thing!" Phil coached. "It's not working!"

Finally the enormous creature pinned Hercules to a cliff with a claw. Thinking quickly, Hercules smashed his fist into the mountain, causing an avalanche that buried him and the Hydra.

Seconds later, Hercules amazed everyone by emerging unharmed from the rubble. The townsfolk went wild. Hercules was their hero!

Overnight, Hercules became a superstar in Thebes. He had battles galore, won them all, and devoted fans followed him everywhere.

Hades was furious. But he knew that Hercules must have a weakness – and he knew that Meg could find out what it was.

Meg didn't want to help Hades. But she had once made a deal with him, trading her freedom to save her ex-boyfriend's life. Now she had to do as he asked. To sweeten the deal, Hades promised to release her if she succeeded.

Meanwhile, Hercules visited Zeus, reenacting some of his victories for his adoring father. But Zeus gently broke the news that Hercules was still not ready to rejoin the other gods on Mount Olympus.

"But I'm the most famous person in all of Greece!" Hercules protested. "I'm an action figure – a star!"

"My boy," said Zeus, "being famous isn't the same as being a true hero. Look inside your heart to discover what you must do."

Later that day, Hercules was thrilled when Meg came to see him. "You look like you've been working too hard," she said. "Do you think your nanny goat would go berserk if you took the afternoon off?"

Hercules eagerly ignored his duties to spend some time with Meg. She questioned him closely to try to discover his weaknesses, but soon realised he had none. Though she would not admit it to herself, Meg was beginning to fall in love with Hercules.

Phil was furious when he found them. Hercules reluctantly left, but he was so starry-eyed that he didn't notice when Phil fell off Pegasus.

Phil was grumbling as he tried to free himself from a briar patch when he heard voices. Peering through the bushes, he saw Hades talking to Meg. Suddenly he realised that Meg was working for Hades.

"I knew that dame was trouble. This is going to break the kid's heart," he said to himself as he raced off to tell Hercules the truth.

What was even worse was that Hades had discovered Hercules *did* have a weakness – and that weakness was Meg.

When Phil found Hercules at the stadium, the young hero couldn't stop talking about how wonderful Meg was.

"Isn't she the brightest, funniest, most amazing girl you ever met?" Hercules gushed.

"Sure, but she's also a fraud," Phil insisted. "The whole thing is some kind of set-up!"

Hercules stubbornly refused to believe him—so Phil told Hercules he was on his own. "I thought you were gonna be the all-time champ, not the all-time *chump*!" said the disappointed trainer as he left.

Hades was becoming desperate. The alignment of the planets was getting nearer all the time. So he thought of a plan, and went to the stadium to talk to Hercules. He tried to play it cool—which wasn't easy for such a hotheaded guy.

"I would be eternally grateful if you would take just one day off from this hero business of yours," Hades said casually. "I mean, monsters, natural disasters… they can wait a day, can't they?"

Worried about people getting hurt, Hercules refused—until Hades revealed Meg, bound at his side.

Now it was Hercules who was forced into making a deal. Hades promised that if he would give up his strength for just a day, Meg would be safe. Hercules agreed, and within seconds his strength was gone. Then Hades revealed that Meg had been working for him all along. Weak and heartbroken, Hercules had to face the awful truth.

51

The planets aligned and Hades freed the Titans from their prison. "What's the first thing you're going to do when you're out?" he bellowed.

"*Destroy Zeus!*" thundered the Rock Titan, the Lava Titan, the Ice Titan, the Tornado Titan and the one-eyed Cyclops as they emerged.

"Good answer!" Hades told them gleefully. Then he sent the Cyclops on a special mission to Thebes, to hunt down Hercules and destroy him.

Hermes the messenger was napping peacefully on a cloud when a loud rumbling shook him awake. His eyes flew open to see the angry Titans approaching Mount Olympus.

"Uh-oh!" he said to himself. "We're in big trouble!"

He raced to tell Zeus, who ordered him to summon the gods for an immediate counterattack. Hephaestus began hammering lightning bolts for weapons, and the other gods prepared themselves for battle. But they were no match for the Tornado Titan, who sucked them up like a vacuum cleaner.

Down on Earth, Thebes was in flames. The Cyclops was destroying everything in his path, and the people were crying out for Hercules.

Though he no longer possessed his incredible strength, Hercules confronted the Cyclops, who simply kicked him away like a pebble. Meg pleaded with Hercules not to continue his fight with the giant, but Hercules no longer cared what happened to him.

Suddenly Meg heard a familiar whinny coming from a nearby stable. It was Pegasus, who had been trapped and tied up by Pain and Panic. Meg freed him, and the two set off in search of Phil.

They found Phil about to board a boat leaving Thebes.

"Hercules gave us something we'd both lost – hope!" Meg reminded him. "Now he's lost *his* hope. You're the only one who can get through to him. If you don't help him now, he'll die!"

Hearing these words, Phil agreed to return to the city with her.

Up on Mount Olympus, Zeus was in trouble. All the gods had been captured, and now he was out of lightning bolts.

"Hades!" exclaimed Zeus when the god of the Underworld appeared. "I should have known *you* were behind this!"

A moment later the Lava Titan arrived and surrounded Zeus with molten rock. To finish the job, the Ice Titan cooled the lava with his frigid breath. Zeus was encased in solid rock, unable to move.

Hercules wasn't faring much better. When Phil and Meg found him, the Cyclops was about to finish him off.

"C'mon, kid, fight back!" Phil pleaded. He encouraged Hercules not to lose sight of his dreams—or his belief in himself.

When he heard Phil's words, Hercules' resolve returned. He grabbed a burning stick and thrust it at the monster. Screaming with pain, the Cyclops dropped Hercules. As the monster staggered blindly, he plunged over a cliff.

Suddenly a column the Cyclops had collided with fell towards Hercules. Meg pushed him out of the way, but was trapped by the column herself. As Hercules tried to free her, his strength returned.

"Hades' deal is broken," Meg explained weakly. "He promised I wouldn't get hurt. You must go to Olympus and stop him." Before he left, Meg finally admitted to Hercules that she loved him.

Hercules rushed to Mount Olympus, breaking the gods' chains and freeing Zeus from the lava. Hephaestus quickly made some new lightning bolts for Zeus, and the gods went back into action.

Zeus and Hercules joined forces. Zeus' lightning bolts held the Titans back while Hercules used the Tornado Titan to gather them up. When the job was done, Hercules hurled the Titans into space.

Amidst the confusion, Hades began to make his getaway. "A friend of yours is *dying* to see me, Wonder Boy!" he shouted to Hercules. Horrified, Hercules realised he meant Meg!

Hercules raced back to Meg's side, but it was too late. The Fates had cut her Thread of Life.

"This wasn't supposed to happen!" Hercules cried in anguish.

"I'm sorry, kid," said Phil sadly. "But there are some things you can't change."

A look of determination came over Hercules' face. "Yes, I *can*," he replied as he mounted Pegasus and raced off to the Underworld.

Hades already had Meg's spirit in the Pit of Death. "You like making deals," Hercules said to him. "Take me in Meg's place." This was an unexpected bonus for Hades, and he quickly agreed.

As Hercules dived to retrieve Meg's spirit, he grew older. But the Fates couldn't cut his Thread of Life. Hercules was a god at last!

Fear shot through Hades when he saw Hercules emerging from the pit with Meg's spirit. "Meg, talk to him," he pleaded. But that made Hercules angrier and he hurled Hades down into the Pit of Death.

Hercules reunited Meg's spirit with her body. Her eyes fluttered open. Zeus lifted the couple to Mount Olympus on a cloud.

"A true hero isn't measured by the size of his strength, but by the strength of his heart," Zeus proclaimed. "Welcome home, son!"

"Father, this is the moment I've always dreamed of," Hercules began. "But a life without Meg – even an immortal one – would be empty. I wish to stay on Earth with her. I know now that it's where I belong."

Zeus and Hera nodded their approval. They would miss their beloved son, but they knew he had found happiness at last.

HERCULES returned to a hero's welcome on Earth. In the cheering crowd were his proud earthly parents, Alcmene and Amphitryon.

Suddenly someone pointed at the sky. There were gasps of wonder as everyone looked up – there, shining in the heavens, was a new constellation, created by Zeus in his son's honour.

So that's how our story ends, folks – full of love and happiness, with Hercules a star in heaven and on Earth. Hercules got his wish, and so did Phil – he had trained a true hero, after all!